LIFE SENTENCE

ALSO BY NINA CASSIAN

POETRY

IN ENGLISH:

Blue Apple, translated by Eva Feiler, 1981

Lady of Miracles, Poems by Nina Cassian, selected and translated from the Romanian by Laura Schiff, 1982

Call Yourself Alive: The Poetry of Nina Cassian, translated from the Romanian by Andrea Deletant and Brenda Walker, 1988

IN ROMANIAN:

On the Scale of One to One (La Scara 1/1), 1947

Our Soul (Sufletul nostru), 1949

Vital Year, 1917 (An viu, nouă sute şi şaptesprezece), 1949

Horea not alone anymore (Horea nu mai este singur), 1952

Youth (Tinerețe), 1953

Selected poems (Versuri alese), 1955

The Measures of the Year (Vîrstele anului), 1957

Dialogue of Wind and Sea (Dialogul vîntului cu marea), 1957

Spectacle in the Open-air—a Monograph of Love, (Spectacol in aer liber—o monografie a dragostei), 1961

Gift Giving (Să ne facem daruri), 1963

The Discipline of the Harp (Disciplina harfei), 1964

The Blood (Sîngele), 1966

Parallel Destinies (Destinele paralele), 1967

Ambit (Ambitus), 1969

Time Devouring: Selected Poems (Cronofagie), 1969

Requiem (Recviem), 1971

The Big Conjugation (Marea conjugare), 1971

Lotto Poems (Loto-poeme), 1972

Suave (Suave), 1974

Spectacle in the Open-air: Selected Love Poems (Spectacol in aer liber), 1974

One Hundred Poems (O sută de poeme), 1975

Orbits (Viraje), 1978

For Mercy (De îndurare), 1981

Count Down (Numărătoarea inversa), 1983

FOR CHILDREN

Fearless Niki (Nică fără frică), 1952

What Oona Saw (Ce-a văzut Oana), 1952

Flowers of One's Country (Florile Patriei), 1954

Puzzled Muzzle (Bot-gros, cățel fricos), 1957

Prince Meow (Pințul Miorlau)

Tusky's Adventures (Aventurile lui Trompişor), 1959

The Mischief Maker (Incurcă-lume), 1961

Rainbow—Selection (Curcubeu), 1962

Tigrino and Tigrene, the Story of Two Tiger Cubs, (Povestea a doi pui de tigru,
  numiți Ninigra și Aligru), 1969

T. V. Cat (Pisica la televizor), 1971

Among Us Children (Intre noi copiii), 1974

Copper-red and the Seven Dachshunds (Roșcată ca arama și cei șapte șoricari)

PUPPET PLAYS

The Curious Little Elephant (After Kipling) (Elefănțelul curios), 1964

The Cat All by Itself (After Kipling) (Pisica de una singură), 1967

Tigrino and Tigrene (Ninigra si Aligru), 1972

Fearless Niki (Nică fără frică), 1984

FICTION

IN ROMANIAN:

You're Terrific—I'm Leaving You: (Atît de grozavă și adio:), 1971

Fictitious Confessions (Confidențe fictive), 1974

Parlor Games (Jocuri de vacanță), 1984

TRANSLATIONS

Mayakovsky, Chukovsky, Aliger, Ritsos, Morgenstern, Molière, Brecht, Shakespeare, Celan,
  Guillevic, and others

LIFE SENTENCE

SELECTED POEMS

NINA CASSIAN

Edited, and with an Introduction by

WILLIAM JAY SMITH

W·W·Norton & Company

New York   London

ACKNOWLEDGMENTS

Translations of certain of these poems appeared first in the following magazines and anthologies: *The American Poetry Review, Cover, Modern Poetry in Translation, Other Voice, Women on War: Essential Voices for the Nuclear Age,* edited by Daniela Gioseffi (Simon and Schuster: A Touchstone Book, 1988), *The World Book of Women Poets, The William and Mary Review, Verse,* and others. Translations of the following poems appeared first in *The New Yorker:* "Ballad of the Jack of Diamonds," "Dead Still," "Farce," "Greed," "The Green Elephant," "Ghosts," "Poetry," "Post-Meridian," "September," "That Animal," "The Widow," "The Young Bat." William Jay Smith's introduction to *Life Sentence* and the following poems appeared first in *The American Poetry Review:* "Self-Portrait," "Tirade," "Game Mistress," "Joyful Sacrifice," "The Couple," "Sacrilege," "Ready for Goodbye," "Extraordinary Performance."

Translations of other poems appeared first in the following collections. The author is grateful to the editors and translators for permission to reprint them: *Lady of Miracles, Poems by Nina Cassian,* selected and translated from the Romanian by Laura Schiff, Berkeley: Cloud Marauder Press, 1982. *Call Yourself Alive: The Poetry of Nina Cassian,* translated from the Romanian by Andrea Deletant and Brenda Walker, London: Forest Books, 1988.

Printed in the United States of America.
The text of this book is composed in 11/13.5 Fairfield Medium,
with display type set in Post Antiqua Bold.
Composition and manufacturing by the Maple-Vail Book Manufacturing Group.
Book design by Margaret M. Wagner. Ornament by Antonia Krass.
First Edition

Library of Congress Cataloging-in-Publication Data
Cassian, Nina.
[Poems. English. Selections]
Life sentence : selected poems / Nina Cassian ; edited, and with
an introduction, by William Jay Smith.—1st ed.
p. cm.
Translated from Romanian.
1. Cassian, Nina—Translations, English. I. Smith, William Jay,
1918– . II. Title.
PC840.13.A9L5 1990
859'.134—dc20   89-33245

ISBN 0-393-02786-4

W. W. Norton & Company, Inc., 500 Fifth Avenue, New York, N. Y. 10110
W. W. Norton & Company Ltd., 37 Great Russell Street, London WC1B 3NU
1 2 3 4 5 6 7 8 9 0

To
HERMANN MAYER
My Prince Protector

CONTENTS

Contents

III   TABLES WIPED CLEAN

IV THE WHEEL NOT IN MY HANDS

V LIFE SENTENCE

Contents

TRANSLATORS

Fleur Adcock

Cristian Andrei

Nina Cassian

Kim Cushman

Andrea Deletant

Marguerite Dorian

Eva Feiler

Dana Gioia

Christopher Hewitt

Barbara Howes

Carolyn Kizer

Stanley Kunitz

Naomi Lazard

Laura Schiff

William Jay Smith

Petre Solomon

Elliott Urdang

Brenda Walker

Ruth Whitman

Richard Wilbur

INTRODUCTION

I

NINA CASSIAN comes to us, even in translation, as a poet of tremendous range and vitality. We are at once aware of her antecedents: a modernist, nurtured on those French poets who, through T. S. Eliot and Ezra Pound, helped to change the shape of twentieth-century poetry in England and America, she is at the same time very much the product of Romania. Her poetry has something of the clear line and the strikingly simple texture of her countryman, Brancusi, and, like him, her sophistication is grounded in folklore. There is great variety to her work and a comic spirit that recalls the theater of the absurd of her other countryman, Ionesco. Her themes are eternal, love and loss, life and death, and they are communicated with an immediacy as rare as it is compelling. Hers is a passionate commitment in the greatest tradition of lyric poetry. For this poet, life is indeed a tragic sentence. But the sentence that she composes in answer to life is made up of clean Latin vowels, with rational syllables "trying to clear the occult mind." Only in poetry does she reach "the word, the inhabited homestead." And in poetry she takes her reader with her.

Nina Cassian composes poetry by "tea-light," in a golden zone of "pure burning amber." And in that golden light she explores the physicality of love. As with Sappho, the sight of the lover is overpowering:

> Your eyes make the air pulse,
> they electrify the house,
> the drawers open, rugs flood
> down the stairs like a river.
> Your star-like teeth
> rip open my heart like lightning.

And when the lover has departed:

> the air whistled as if clutching a line
> of a thousand arrows never reaching their target.

and the cruelty of the departed lover circles the poet's head "like a bright rotting halo." Rejected in love, the poet feels her arms like anchors trail at her side and she chokes on an "Isadora-scarf" of smoke from her cigarette:

> Void. Loneliness . . .
> search is pointless—
> all that is true
> are my doubts:
> How real are you?
> How real were you?

Everything in Cassian's poetry has its precise sensory description:

> A rug of dead butterflies at my feet,
> dead and limp
> (they don't experience rigor mortis).

The widow smells "incitingly/of absence:"

> A dog sniffs at her solitude
> and takes off yelping.

The memory of childhood is intense and physical:

> Even now my breast bone's aching
> when I remember how I was running
> because the smell of petunias invaded everything.

Her poems are filled with creatures—birds, domestic, exotic, and fantastic—with squirrels, rabbits, monkeys. Hers is a living, moving world (the poet is in orbit), where even the smallest sensation is penetrating and where she is "deafened by dust falling on the furniture," and where she experiences love in

long knives in the night,
beaks by the window . . .

and sees terror

in the long, rough, white thread
through aunt's needle—
the fly's legs rubbing against each other.

The wheel of the ship on which she finds herself stranded

rests like a spider
fixed on my wooden sky . . .

Even the poet's devotion to language is precise and physical; she speaks
of the

clitoris in my throat
vibrating, sensitive, pulsating,
exploding in the orgasm of Romanian.

   For all the immediacy of Nina Cassian's poetry (and this immedi-
acy and sensory appeal have made her a brilliant writer for children),
her tone is never confessional but rather intense and direct and with-
out self-pity. In her celebrated "Self-Portrait" she compares her strange
triangular face to the figurehead on the prow of a pirate ship. She is
vulnerable but proud; her totem bird is the swan, but a swan with a
big bill, half-bird, half-woman, graceful and mysterious. Nina Cas-
sian's friend Petre Solomon has given us this description of the poet
when she first began to publish:

Although she had not yet published her verses in a volume, Nina's
poems in various magazines of the time signaled a characteristically
lyrical voice—it was strong and acute, in harmony with her whole

iconoclastical generation. To her outstanding intelligence, an inimit-able gift for cutting and explosive statement could be added. Equally talented in poetry, music, and painting (she had taken classes from Löwendal and Maxy), Nina even had an extraordinary gift for acting in public or during our literary sessions in the circle of her numerous intimate friends. Nina's presence in a group of otherwise heteroge-neous individuals acted always as a unifying factor, as a social "glue" of immediate effect. It was enough that she appear among such a group for everyone to become lively, as they discovered elective affinities. Improvising or playing Debussy, Bartók, or Constantin Silvestri on the piano, Nina would find herself the center of attention, which she could also capture through other means, especially brilliant conversation. Having a complex because of her Dantesque profile, Nina always tried to prove the superiority of her intellect in an aggressive manner, devised to disarm those who might have been paying heed to her "ugliness" (which was in fact mostly imaginary).

When I first met her in Bucharest in 1970, I found Nina Cassian very much the center of her circle, as Petre Solomon describes her, a charming and witty companion, but not in the least aggressively intellectual. Nor did I find anything ugly in her Dantesque profile: on the contrary, it seemed only to enhance her charm and elegance and to make her totally unlike anyone else.

I I

NINA CASSIAN (Renée Annie Ştefănescu) was born November 27, 1924, at Galati, a city on the Danube. She would discover the charm of this city later during several short vacations because her family moved when she was two years old to Brasov, an ancient city at the base of Mount Timpa in Transylvania. It was here that Coresi in 1560 published a Romanian translation of the *Gospels,* the first major book in Romanian. "Brasov provided me," Nina Cassian has written, "with an ideal setting, the halo of an Austro-Hungarian 'burg': heavy wooden gates concealing mysterious interior courtyards; the majestic Black Church; narrow lanes paved with stones from the river climbing toward the mountain—and green mists on the wooded peaks; sumptuous winters; cold, sparkling well springs; glades with translucent flowers; strong downpours; vivid, scented air. I was a happy child." The town had a mixed population of Romanians, Germans, Hungarians, and Jews. "I moved among all these different peoples, learning their languages and making friends," she continues. "It is not too farfetched to think that it was this eclectic background that molded my internationalist feeling, never allowing me to lose a sense of the specific character of the respective peoples—quite the contrary—and protecting me from any prejudices and chauvinist narrowmindedness. As a child, this amounted to observing every religious holiday as it came along so that the whole year was for me a perpetual celebration. I was particularly fond of the celebration of the Saint Nicholas of Austrian tradition. I enjoyed setting my little shoes on the windowsill and in the morning finding them brimming over with candies and, especially, with scarlet cellophane bags from which little red velvet devils holding tiny golden pitchforks were grinning at me. Of course, I waited with equal impatience for the ceremony of trimming the Christmas tree and for Easter, with its snowdrops, chocolate rabbits, and little eggs of blue, pink, purple sugar. My parents were not religious so even the Jewish traditions that were preserved in our home had for me a quality of entertaiment and culinary ecstasy rather than of spiritual fulfillment."

When she was five years old, she had her first piano lessons and composed her first waltz; she also learned to read and wrote her first poem. Her parents had little formal education but her father became a reputable translator from French and German and the author of a fine version of Poe's "The Raven." She went through the primary grades in the Jewish school affiliated with the Synagogue of Brasov; her summers were spent in Constanta, where she discovered a beach "still savage and abundant with giant dunes, and the multicolored atmosphere of a cosmopolitan city, the bead curtains at the entrances of the barber shops, the cafés, the wave-washed piers, the harbor, the statue of Ovid who found himself exiled to these inhospitable shores when Constanta was still called Tomi and in whose cold winters wine would freeze in goblets."

When she was eleven, her family moved to Bucharest, where her father was unemployed for a long period of time and where the family moved from boarding house to boarding house, each one shabbier than the last. She began her high-school studies at the Pompilian Institute, where French was taught intensively. It was a school for young ladies of good families but which occasionally accepted a few of more modest backgrounds. She was an unexceptional student, having no appetite for disciplined study with the exception of foreign languages, music and drawing, subjects that would always salvage her grade average. When Romania embraced Fascism, she was expelled from the Pompilian Institute and required to register at a high school for Jewish girls. While still a student, she became an ardent Communist, embracing a doctrine that she felt promised to solve all problems. "I am not the only person in history," she has said, "who came to see an ideal turned into its very opposite."

In January 1943, at the age of eighteen, she married Vladimir (Jany) Colin, a handsome young Jewish Communist poet and an admirer of modern, especially French, poetry. But in 1948, when she was 23 she met Al. I. (Ali) Ştefănescu, a Christian ten years older than she, a thin, wrinkled little man ("the old Child" he had been called when young), who had been orphaned at the age of nine. He had worked his way through the university to become a teacher of French and an editor of the review, *Contemporanul,* and later a critic and novelist. She divorced Colin and married Ştefănescu. It was perhaps the total difference in their backgrounds that intensified the magnetism that drew them together and kept them together for three and a half decades until his death.

After the turmoil of World War II and just before meeting Ştefănescu, Nina Cassian published her first book, *On the Scale of One to One,* a volume inspired by the *poètes fantaisistes,* Max Jacob, Toulet, and Apollinaire. Cassian had already translated a number of French poets as well as the *Gallow Songs* of Christian Morgenstern. In her teens, when she began to write seriously, Cassian had been influenced by Mihai Eminescu (1850–89), the great Romantic, and later by Tudor Arghezi (1880–1967), whose rich metaphorical language held her attention. But, as with many other Romanian poets, it was the work of Ion Barbu (1885–1961), that truly revolutionized her style. Barbu, a mathematician, whose real name was Dan Barbilian, was as hermetic as Mallarmé and as original. Barbu's work, as well as that of the French poets she emulated, led her in this early volume to a concentrated form of surrealism. There are surrealist touches throughout the work of Nina Cassian, but she has made it clear that she never wholly espoused surrealist doctrine. Her surrealism is close to that found in Romanian folklore. Like Ionesco, Nina Cassian owes something to Urmuz (1883–1923), whose rich burlesque spirit inspired the surrealists. The Castle Nevermore in her poem is straight out of Edgar Allan Poe, but it is also rooted in Transylvania, the home of Vlad the Impaler, the fifteenth-century Prince of Wallachia. Vampires flicker through her poetry, which is replete at times with blood and terror, but is often edged with gallows humor, and, more often than not, with a touch of the absurd.

Because of her first book, Nina Cassian was attacked by the authorities as an enemy of the people. She tried to change her style and follow the party line. She cut back on her vocabulary and attempted to use only words that the masses could understand with no metaphorical language whatever. And yet similes would appear all the same. In one poem she described Lenin sitting at his desk while the light filtering through the window turned his inkwell into a great blue light bulb. The poem caused a scandal: she was accused of wishing to write about the ink and the light bulb and of using Lenin merely as a pretext. With sincerity and conviction, she wrote four more books, which she now rejects aesthetically. Her conscience was clear, but her talent was in eclipse. What fantasy she had left went into her books for children, in which she could indulge her word play. Finally between 1955 and 1957 she found that she could not write at all. She turned for a while to composing; musical notes, she said, could not be found in the dictionary and she could not be accused of making allusions in her musical compositions.

In 1957 there was a thaw; Stalin had died. "Words I had banished and despised came back to me little by little," Nina has said. "Then it was an avalanche—books, books, books, one after another. And again, poetry. We had five wonderful years from 1965 to 1970. We enjoyed an amazing freedom, and we all used this freedom to write as we wished." The seventies, however, were more restricted and more chaotic. Nina Cassian turned again to musical composition, but continued to publish poetry, children's books, and film criticism.

I I I

WHEN Nina Cassian came to this country in 1985, it never occurred to her that she might not return to Romania. Invited to teach a course in Creative Writing at New York University, she arrived in September and began the semester with every indication that her stay here would be a pleasant one. Her husband of many years, Al. I. Ştefǎnescu, had died several months before, and she welcomed the change of scene and the challenge of meeting and working with American writers and students. She was informed almost at once that she would receive the Fulbright fellowship which had been awarded to her earlier but which the Romanian authorities had never told her about. After such a happy beginning, she found within two months that it would be impossible under any circumstances to return to Romania.

During the summer of 1985, her friend of many years, Gheorghe Ursu, an engineer and amateur of the arts, had been questioned by the police and had ultimately been set free. Ursu was an old friend; Nina Cassian had shared summer vacations with him in a fishing village, of which she has spoken in her reminiscences of Paul Celan. They had often joked and shared, as old friends do, their feelings about literature, life, and the political scene. In New York Nina Cassian heard that Ursu had again been arrested. In his office the police had discovered a diary that he had kept for forty years. It was an important, expressive, thorough document, in which he had put down every aspect of his life, and in which he had committed the indiscretion of mentioning his close friends by name. Nina Cassian learned that she was not only named but that pointed satirical and often scathing verses in which she had lampooned the authorities had been carefully copied out and their author clearly identified. As a result, Ursu, she learned, had been questioned in detail about her. He had subsequently been tortured, and after another month, he died. It was clear that now she could not return to Bucharest. "A poet never leaves his country, his territory, his language, of his or her own free will," Nina Cassian has told me, "but I had no choice." She requested political asylum in this country, and her request was granted.

The nightmare that she had delineated so splendidly in her poems—the ship of her country dead-still in the water with no helmsman to guide it, the syllables of the lie outlined on the leader's lips—were no longer merely imaginative projections; they were absolute reality. Argue with chaos though she might, in poetry she had won but in life she had lost. Her life sentence, like death itself, was confirmed when at Christmas 1987, she learned that the authorities had put a seal on the house that she had left behind in Bucharest; they had emptied it of all its contents, all her manuscripts, letters, drawings, paintings, notebooks, musical compositions, her entire library and her most precious personal mementos from her school days and her travels, the entire accumulation of a rich and full literary life. What has happened to all these things no one knows. She has been written out of her country's literature, its anthologies, its histories, its textbooks. Her books, even her totally apolitical children's books, have all been withdrawn from circulation. At present she is a nonperson; she does not exist. As in one of her poems, the tables have been wiped clean. The only other similar instance in recent literary history that I know of is that of Aldous Huxley, who watched his house in the hills above

Los Angeles burn to the ground with all the writings he had retained since his boyhood together with the journals that his wife had kept during her entire life. Like Nina, Huxley was beginning life again, *tabula rasa*. But Nina was beginning life again in another country, with another language very different from her own. It would not be an easy adjustment.

When I was in Bucharest again last February, I saw a number of the friends of Nina Cassian who had surrounded her on my previous visit in 1970. Her absence left a terrible gap. Without her, something of the cultural fabric of her country, of which she had been so vital a part, seemed to have come unglued.

IV

BECAUSE Nina Cassian is herself a brilliant translator, she has understood the difficulty of assembling this selection of her poems in English. Some poems have had to be omitted because the resonance and the allusions of the original could not be carried over. Nina Cassian often employs intricate verse forms, rich in rhymes. Richard Wilbur and Dana Gioia have succeeded brilliantly in retaining exactly the rhyme schemes of the poems they have translated; and many others have also given close approximations of the original form. But because rhyme is much more difficult in English than in Romanian, some translators have had to abandon it completely in order to convey the force and meaning of the original poem. The author has permitted, and even encouraged, her translators to take considerable liberty as long as they did not violate the spirit of her work. It is surely a tribute to the validity of Nina Cassian's poetry that that spirit has come through so well in so many of the versions of these poet-translators, each with his or her own distinctive style.

WILLIAM JAY SMITH
New York
February 1989

I

THE TROUBLED BAY

ON AN OLD THEME

When daylight colors fade, the night appears.
When night recedes, it leaves the day behind.
This alternating tide of colors
can strike a person blind.

Such perilous attractions: Don't climb on green.
It proves an iceberg that's so dangerous
that slipping off you'll drown in the rank red
that's boiling under all of us.

Don't stir up purple. Leave some mystery
intact and undisturbed. But don't ignore
your longing for the orange of lighted windows
that shine beside your childhood door.

I've witnessed people murdered by the white
refusals of a sheet, and men I know
went mad from sending printed yellow forms
to emperors who died long ago.

Every now and then you can depend
at least on either blue or indigo.
But no one ever mentions black—except
when there is nowhere else to go.

(DANA GIOIA)

THE BIRDS ARE WHITE AND TRIANGULAR

The birds are white and triangular.
The dog's head is orange and triangular.
My head is sad and triangular.
The wrinkle in the left corner of my mouth is slanted.
The wrinkle in the right corner of my mouth is vertical.
The white birds fly, drown, revive.
The dog's head is proud like that of an eagle.
My head is long like the head of a dog.

(LAURA SCHIFF)

ECSTASY

On the moon's stripe the goldfish meet.
Look, a mad piling mass,
tails dissolving like soft snow.
In the cold gold wine of the sea, giddy.
A pale mute frenzy flows from their mouths.
Goldfish in gold wine, in magic moon,
noiselessly drunk,
glide past the drum of the ear, the air,
and etch with tails digits of light.
A dazzling swarm drowns.
Their bulging eyes repeat the moon
a thousand times scattered in waves, a thousand clusters of
grapes, grapes, grapes, grapes, grapes.

(LAURA SCHIFF)

MEMORIES

There are nights when the very walls expand
and open slowly out to fairyland. . . .

When all is diaphanous, light, and blue
as if the heart of a brook were pouring through.

Windows quiver; colors are wet and clear;
a pebble sparkles—with a sparkle one can hear.

If only this magical moment would always stay
when pain with the sunset strangely ebbs away.

Thank you, childhood, thank you for this light
that cuts through our grown-up sleep, our adult night.

(WILLIAM JAY SMITH)

PART OF A BIRD

Even now my breast bone's aching
when I remember how I was running
because the smell of petunias invaded everything.
Ah, God, how warm it was around
my legs, bare, long and free
and evening fell over the sea,
over a crowd, gathered there, and over
the strange deserted pavilion
where we played and I
didn't even think about my ugly head
and other children hadn't noticed it either
because we were all running too fast instead
so the transparent eagle of evening wouldn't get us
and the hum of adults from the street
and the sea, the sea, which threatened (protected?)
that *fine del primo tempo.*

It was forever summer, a light summer
a summer of water and sandals, immune
to that alcohol, soon to be called Love,
—and in the deserted pavilion (in vain you'd look for it,
it's either been removed with two fingers
from its ring of earth by War, or by some
useful work, or else forgotten)
we were playing childhood, but, in fact,
I can't remember anyone, I don't think
there was another child apart from me,
because, see, I can only remember
a lonely flight into mystery
staged by the gestures of the sea, I remember
only the happiness, oh God, of leaning
with bare arms and legs on warm stones,
of sloping ground, with grass,
of the innocent air of evening.

Flowers smelled dizzily in that place
where, a little above men and women,
who definitely smelled of tobacco,
hot barbecue and beer, I
was running, unaware of my ugly head,
breaking, in fact, the soft head from the flower
and kissing it on the lips
while the sea also smelled more strongly
than now, it was wilder, its seaweed
darker, and cursed the rocks
even more in the way it whipped them.
It wasn't far from home
to that place, I could run there
and back and no one would miss me,
in four steps and eight jumps I was there,
but, first, I stole from fences
feathers of peacocks left between slats,
most beautiful feathers I've not seen since
with the immense blue green eye
and with golden eyelashes so long
that I was holding a whole bird in my hands
not part of one
and I was tearing at feathers
stuck between slats
tearing at something from the mystery
of those fiendish courtyards
and then I was running toward that deserted pavilion
from the edge of the sea
and I was running round it and through it
through derelict rooms
where mad martins battered themselves against walls,
with the ceiling bursting outside and in, as if within me.

I wore a short sleeveless dress
the color of sand when sun runs out of strength

and in the autumn I should have gone to school,
and the performance of the sea kept breaking my rib cage
to make me more roomy, that's why
my heart was beating and even now the cage in my
                                        chest hurts
at the memory of that beat of the sea
while attempting to enter me
especially at evening when flowers fade
without losing their color completely,
staying pink with tea, violet with milk,
losing only their stems in the darkness,
floating, beheaded, at a certain height
above the grass which had also vanished.
This is a tremendous memory,
absolutely unforgettable,
the feeling of a light, unchained body,
invulnerable, perfect, my head
just a natural extension of it,
supervising only its speed and orientation.
Yet I never hurt myself,
I can't remember ever having fallen that summer.
I was light, extremely healthy,
inspired, and if I wasn't flying
it was only because I preferred to run on earth
and not for any other reason.

And after that . . .
What was I saying? Ah, yes, I had long bare legs
and bare slender arms
and in the deserted pavilion there was this strange coolness
as if an invisible sea had breezed through it . . .

And after that . . .
—Where was I? Ah, yes, the flowers full of night . . .
like sacred smoke

and my lonely flight
through gentle and benevolent mysteries . . .

And after that?

(*BRENDA WALKER AND ANDREA DELETANT*)

THE BURNING OF THE FAMOUS
CASTLE NEVERMORE

Nobody noticed when suddenly the lights went on.
"It's terrifying how clearly I see," the old aunt cried.
Among family portraits and silver, alone untouched,
the blind butler by the door stood paralyzed.

Through the burning bulbs a threatening gala swept;
the guests excused themselves and departed all,
leaving behind in a stand in the entrance hall
four canes and a gray dog no one recognized.

From the wall quicksilver-like Revelation shone;
beneath the parquet droned an electric heart.
Fainting dead away, the old aunt tore the curtains apart,
and on the horizon the castle burned and burned.

(WILLIAM JAY SMITH)

THE COUPLE

Necks crossed, then parallel,
they float in slow motion
white and hazel
mingling their blond contrasts,
their floating heads
watching the world from lunar heights,
their fragile legs like antennae,
the bones of their foreheads
breathing sadness and exile
as they circle in their dismal arena,
straining upward to escape
as if pulled by invisible leashes
in love with their heads
but hating their captive bodies.
They separate, they follow
like the languid hours
of the final days
of an extinct species—
giraffes!

(CHRISTOPHER HEWITT)

EVOLUTION

Today a grandly furious storm
hurled a pile of mussels at my feet,
reminding me of the first creation.
O sea, that element in which I was born.

Cradle of life, long convoy
of sea anemones, reptiles
and scaly monsters, winding toward us
imprisoned in our sweet and fragile forms . . .

I came from the sea and to the sea
I would return, to be immersed in her story,
ever lost and everlasting.
Black mussels on the shore: memento mori.

(STANLEY KUNITZ)

THE INCLINED PLANE

Up, up, with an as yet undefined movement
probably called translation—have you ever seen
the infinite procession of slaves carrying enormous blocks
which, for their part, will for all time
bear the majestic name of pyramids?
Down, down, have you ever felt the first breath
of the avalanche, the delicate slivers and dust,
barely moving, ingenuous, putting forth a gesture
                                    of destruction
and beginning to shake the world's foundations?
A single plane, inclined—toward what?
Toward the x-axis,
toward the y-axis,
and all the other conventions,
toward something rising and something falling;
the slope alone—you can clamber up or slide down.

Do you remember gliding on a gray tongue of concrete
toward the green glottis of the sea?
Do you remember touching the surface of that sea,
                                    and breaking it,
going down through it, feeling a perpetual slope,
                                    an inclined plane?
It takes a long time to crawl back up and break the surface
because time, there in the depths, has no orifices,
                                    no nostrils, no pores:
it is an obdurate time—a kind of eternity.

Slides, chutes, inclined planes, oh, tragedies—
for tragedies are not obligatory; they are tragic
precisely because they could have been avoided—
so neither the vertical nor the horizontal really exists—
only a great inclined plane.

Have you ever struggled to get up with your fingers
clenched in the mud that lies between you
                    and the horizon above?
You looked at that pure, cold, cutting skyline
and quickly at the earth in front of your mouth,
then again at the horizon, and at the short blades of grass
that spring between the fingers clenched in that mud.
You fell and struggled again on that treacherous slope
without any other point of support but your own elbows,
kneecaps, heels, and your own forehead
soiled with earth mysteriously like an old manuscript.

The great plane rocks back and forth,
at one end a king, at the other a boar,
at one end a huge block of salt and at the other a book,
at one end a house, on the other a river,
and finally the great plane
rocks with old people and snowfalls,
padlocks, watches, blue leaves, melodic scepters,
horses and ships swinging, death's temples rocking, rocking,
quiet alcohols reeling, balancing.

I stand crucified on a plank, aware
                    of the continual flow of life.
And here I am, incapable of stepping twice
                    into the same stream.
I myself am beginning to pour forth like a spring,
                    my hands prolonging themselves,
my hair, the tail of my eye, flowing down,
then up onto an inclined plane,
my whole being in a procession of ovoid cells, pulsating,
existing, not existing, ending briskly, continuing smoothly—
have you ever seen a floating cross?

It is a bird flying obliquely
over the oblique axis of the globe.
I rest my head in my left palm,
slightly inclined, contemplating, contemplating
The Great Inclined Plane.

(*NAOMI LAZARD*)

GAME MISTRESS

The word was uttered: let us break its neck.
It was better to be silent and far less certain.
The fly used to cut through our boredom with its buzz,
then sprawled across our hands and stained the curtain.

Call out the police to have us carted away.
We have sinned: from now on, stale bread and water. Cheers!
Our relatives tomorrow will arrive with a razor
to cut off our inheritance from our fingers and ears.

So we shall dream tonight about blue rats
and we shall be visibly much paler than before.
Of all the keys, the two really sacred ones
I have hidden in the pocket of my pinafore.

One opens the box that holds the revolvers,
those noisy silencers, there, at rest on the shelf;
the other one doesn't fit any lock whatever.
It's a philosophical key, a Key in Itself.

(*NINA CASSIAN*)

BALLAD OF THE JACK OF DIAMONDS

Here is the Jack of Diamonds, clad
In the rusty coat he's always had,
His two dark brothers wish him dead,
As does the third, whose hue is red.

Here is the Jack of Diamonds, whom
The fates have marked for certain doom.
He is a mediocre fellow,
A scrawny jack whose chest is hollow
And spattered with a dismal yellow—
No model for a Donatello.

The two dark brothers of this jack,
Abetted by the third, alack,
(Who, draped in hearts from head to foot,
Is the most knavish of the lot),
Have vowed by all means to be free
Of him who gives them symmetry,
Making a balanced set of four
Whose equilibrium they abhor.

One brother, on his breast and sleeves,
Is decked with tragic, spadelike leaves.
The next has crosses for décor.
The motif of the third is gore.

The Jack of Diamonds is dead,
Leaving a vacuum in his stead.

This ballad seems at least twice-told.
Well, all Romanian plots are old.

(RICHARD WILBUR)

VACATION

The sea abandoned two blue bodies on the shore.
They could have generated many stars.
They were—they told us—our bodies,
and good folk tried to lay us out.

The blue color wasn't easy to remove.
The night came—color killer—
The moon hurried, like that old new moon,
to pour liquor quickly before thirsty dawn took her.

Finally, discolored, we woke—and loved.
An orange monocle rose from the sea's waistcoat.
High time to look like all the others.
We boiled in oil the last aristocratic fishes.

And in the town of rare trees and light bulbs
dressed alike and put on spectacles.

(BRENDA WALKER AND ANDREA DELETANT)

DIALOGUE OF THE WIND AND THE SEA

He: I am the unknown traveler
       Without a face, on the fields of the horizon.
       Huge birds thrash in my hair.
       I'm the enemy of immobility.

She: Wind, I don't want to be disturbed. Not yet.
       I'm frightened by that voice: yours.
       Don't smash my young body on the rocks.
       Wind, no. Not yet.

He: In sleep, in salt, you have time to return
       to your bed of languid sand.
       But I want to sing your green triumph
       with a thousand trumpets, beautiful one.

She: I'm in turmoil. I tense my water muscles.
       So much love makes me sing!
       Fluid, high, I abandon my bed
       To become wind, to become wind!

(RUTH WHITMAN)

THE MASTER AND MARGARITA

Near the flower Marguerite
sits the tomcat Behemoth.
The flower is illiterate,
Behemoth is polyglot.

Yellow is the daisy's eye,
yellow is the tomcat's eye.
In so many strange events,
candor and maleficence.

Held together close and tight,
on secluded page they meet—
Eternal couple: Wrong and Right—
Behemoth and Marguerite.

(WILLIAM JAY SMITH)

CEREMONY OF ZERO WEATHER

Up until the end, she will gnaw
the floorboards of the house she'll enter,
the Mother Mouse, her belly full,
female bowing to destiny, on that St. Nicholas Day
forty little mice she'll put forth,
fine presents for the children.

The tribe of cellar citizens multiplies
during the winter holidays while at the stream
mass the white tubs, virgin-color;
candles now are all that melt
when tiny devils make sparks fly
from the horns and from the hooves.

In place of devils mice cavort
in the bags of cellophane
where a diaphanous sugar snows—
when the wee bags start marching,
this evening the whole town becomes
a sacred scarlet spectacle.

And the little ones' teeth chatter,
under the bed the youngsters hide,
afraid of growing up all of a sudden.
But beneath the bed, the Mother Mouse
squeezes them against her gray belly,
strangles them there without a sound.

(BARBARA HOWES AND KIM CUSHMAN)

THE TROUBLED BAY

The lighthouse there at Cape Crepuscular
sends out signals: the weather is getting rough.
The rock on which it stands has its throat cut off
under the streaming white of its foam-foulard.

What is the water saying? Lies. Lies.
Don't look for solid ground to become immune.
The bay is unsafe; everything is a disguise;
the masts make the sign of the cross upon the moon.

I knew, as I swam at length far out from shore,
thinking of poets and so much in their debt,
having absorbed a hundred poems or more,
I'd have to write, or drown in one, myself.

(NINA CASSIAN AND WILLIAM JAY SMITH)

CONTROVERSY

I wrote a poem, an oblique poem,
a kind of calligram, I mean.
Someone said it was an equation
being solved behind a screen.

Another laughed and said: It's a broom;
it is just a broom, I swear.
The third one cried: A tree, a tree,
tossing its oranges into the air.

No one knew what the poem was.
But the Plastic Artist understood
and thereon deflated a world of rubber
to construct a world of wood.

(WILLIAM JAY SMITH)

II

BURNING
AMBER

TEMPTATION

Call yourself alive? Look, I promise you
that for the first time you'll feel your pores opening
like fish mouths, and you'll actually be able to hear
your blood surging through all those lanes,
and you'll feel light gliding across the cornea
like the train of a dress. For the first time
you'll be aware of gravity
like a thorn in your heel,
and your shoulder blades will ache for want of wings.
Call yourself alive? I promise you
you'll be deafened by dust falling on the furniture,
you'll feel your eyebrows turning to two gashes,
and every memory you have—will begin
at Genesis.

(*BRENDA WALKER AND ANDREA DELETANT*)

KISSES

Our kisses, hundreds, thousands—
even millions—who knows!
I never counted them:
my fruits, squirrels, carnations,
rivers—my knives!
I could sleep and dream on your mouth,
sing and die there,
again and again;
that mouth—deep harbor
for a night's lodging after a long journey,
reaching it, yet still longing to reach it . . .

They're battles—our kisses—
heavy, slow, hurtful,
where blood, voice and memory all take part.
Oh, how jealous I am of the water you drink
and of the words you speak—
of your blue sighs . . .
Jealous of those unjust
partings of our mouths!

(*BRENDA WALKER AND ANDREA DELETANT*)

GREED

I am greedy. Puritans scold me
for running breathlessly
over life's table of contents
and for wishing and longing for everything.

They scold me for feasting
on joy and despair, together
with jugs of sour cream
and hot polenta.

They object to my wearing a tie pin
and a carnation in my hair,
for being sometimes boy, sometimes girl,
and who knows what else!

They rebuke me for not distributing love
according to a plan, for not rationing it,
for having a potter's agile hands
and now and then solving equations.

Well, that's my way! I'm hungry, I'm thirsty,
I rush through the world like a living sound.
I refuse to walk slowly, to crawl,
or to remain indebted for a kiss.

I'm greedy, I gulp things down, I fly,
and I'm proud that on my small lapel
occasionally a decoration glitters—
call it rapture, that golden rosette.

(*STANLEY KUNITZ*)

LONGING

Oh, my love
heavy anchor
hold me tight:
everything hurts,
mouth—from longing,
eyes—from light.

Winds have dropped—
maybe not,
but in the skies
silence reigns,
powerless
heaven sighs.

No more dreams
of steps in snow,
of foxes' traces,
no more flowers—
their hidden souls
sleep in bulbs.

Void. Loneliness . . .
search is pointless—
all that is true
are my doubts:
How real are you?
How real were you?

(BRENDA WALKER AND ANDREA DELETANT)

BREAD AND WINE

We said there'd be a celebration . . .
There wasn't.
And so I dressed for no apparent
reason in the height of fashion.

I waited for you till dawn.
All night I waited.
In the carafe—stagnant wine,
on the tables—stale bread.

And when day came upon the land
—and I knew it would remain there—
I took the flowers from my hair
with a withered hand.

(BRENDA WALKER AND ANDREA DELETANT)

THEY CUT ME IN TWO

They cut me in two, the river and the moon,
and from my mouth the night pours forth like blood.
I am cut in two, I who once was one;
I didn't know that rocks could be so cruel.

With a flower about to open in each eye,
and a blue wind circling me, I stood alone.
The good earth sang to me, "You will not die!"
and my flesh resounded on its lyre of bone.

As with an ax I am severed by nightmare;
the river and the moon cut me in two.
"Once I was one," I cry. "Once I was entire—"
And the part with my head
                          I now rock to and fro.

(WILLIAM JAY SMITH)

PAIN

God, how they shrieked,
how they sobbed
the night birds.
God, how they cackled!
Wide-eyed,
I stared into the dark,
and on every rooftop,
the sea birds
clacked their beaks.
What an orgy of laughter!
The cold jeers
searched for me
in the solitude.
God, how they cackled,
strange city dwellers,
the night birds.
This is pain,
I told myself, keeping vigil.
This is how it hurts.
Deafening
silver wings,
voices, beaks, claws,
long knives in the night,
beaks by the window . . .
. . . you were far
our love over.

(LAURA SCHIFF)

I WANTED TO STAY IN SEPTEMBER

I wanted to stay in September
on that pale deserted beach.
I wanted to cram myself
with ashes from my unfaithful cranes
and let the slow, heavy wind
fall asleep in my long hair
like water in the trawl:
One night I wanted to light
a cigarette, whiter than the moon,
with no one around—just the sea
with its solemn, hidden force;
I wanted to stay in September,
witnessing the passage of time,
with one hand in the trees—the other
in the graying sand, to slip
along with summer into autumn . . .

But it seems my fate's cast
for more dramatic exits,
fated to be uprooted from landscapes
with an unprepared soul,
as I'm fated to quit loving
while still hired to love.

(BRENDA WALKER AND ANDREA DELETANT)

IT WAS A LOVE

It was a love like a chord from Bach,
of such pure gravity . . . Once our movements
had a noble analyzed quality
like pieces in a chess game.

Now here you are in total disorder, alien to laws,
no longer sealing your syllables on my mouth
or caressing my shoulder. You don't even put your palms
over my forehead flushed with ideas.

I can't lose time like this any longer,
forced to feel pain—ashamed to respond.
I breathe deeply: Listen to another chord
that'll take me higher than you—and beyond.

(BRENDA WALKER AND ANDREA DELETANT)

STAINED-GLASS WINDOW

I came here to be with you in winter's crystal—
as in a stained-glass window
ancient couples of kings and queens.
I counted the even trees on the way to your home.
The snow was sumptuous, magic, as in a ballad.

I knocked at the gate. Its wood was cold.
Everywhere absence—like a new
and total winter. The sweet prince
—nowhere . . . with both hands
I took snow and drank
that white place you'd never crossed.

(BRENDA WALKER AND ANDREA DELETANT)

IT IS EVENING, MY LOVE

It is evening, my love.
I don't want to say anything
but that it is an evening made of aromas
which only rain knows how to make happen in nature
                    after a long drought.
On such evenings the docile logs
bake in the cinders though it is spring
with white flowers hanging over
                    the rim of the glass.

It is evening, my love.
I imagine one of your arms around my shoulders
and one of your voices,
which makes me think of a bird cutting
                    the most delicate branch
with the most delicate saw.
—I wonder why its chirp doesn't rust in the rain.

(NAOMI LAZARD)

INTIMACY

I can be alone,
I know how to be alone.

There is a tacit understanding
between my pencils
and the trees outside;
between the rain
and my luminous hair.

The tea is boiling:
my golden zone,
my pure burning amber.

I can be alone,
I know how to be alone.
By tea-light
I write.

(EVA FEILER AND NINA CASSIAN)

READY FOR GOODBYE

Ready for goodbye, although the moon is rising.
Ready for goodbye, although the tea is boiling.
Ready for goodbye, although the wind is pouring
its triumphant notes into the air.
Ready for goodbye, although my sister's mother
carries in her womb a lovely daughter.
Ready for goodbye.

(WILLIAM JAY SMITH)

DREAM GIRL

I entered that room of yours
and put myself near the books,
a delicate statuette
with diamond nails.

During the night I began
to sparkle, to sparkle,
and your familiar sleep
became unnatural.

Then I leapt down onto the cover,
dividing myself into seven pieces,
into seven solitudes
with a resounding center.

And your familiar sleep
splintered into seven fragments,
and lips became transparent
in a kiss.

That's how we wandered through heaven,
seven times seven . . .

—Really?
—No, just a dream. Just a dream.

(BRENDA WALKER AND ANDREA DELETANT)

BECAUSE YOU DON'T LOVE ME

I smile, and feel my feeble grin
drip like a blood-streak down my chin
because you don't love me.

I dance, and my heavy hands just trail
like a pair of anchors. I am pale
because you don't love me.

I light a cigarette, and choke
in an Isadora-scarf of smoke
because you don't love me.

(FLEUR ADCOCK)

GERUNDIVE

Eye's corner lengthening . . .
mouth's wrinkle deepening . . .
star's body darkening . . .
man's forehead challenging . . .
dust's horizon hardening . . .
greed's great claw sharpening . . .
sunflower setting . . .

(NINA CASSIAN)

BURNING

I burned in the green oven,
he in the black.
Our fires hated each other
like rival tribes.

Yet when we issued through the chimneys,
our two columns of smoke
worshipped the same idol,
died the same death.

(CHRISTOPHER HEWITT)

THE FIRST AND LAST NIGHT OF LOVE

1

Wolves, snow, and the amazement of being together
made them very silent. Among the trees
their old bodies lay in wait—old eyes
with old glances, refusing to believe they'd ever been
forgotten—were they—forgotten?
Weren't they merely a succession,
wearing numerous heads,
always agreeing and nodding in unison,
weren't their arms more infinite,
and far more significant than those of
familiar and frightening oriental statues?
In the silence one could hear their soft murmuring,
a dispute in the intimacy of cells,
while the night strangled pursuers
with her firm grip.

2

They were aware of one thing only: the start
of their first night of love. They'd entered
a set specially designed, a room
where sinister paintings had been removed,
a cat with a mouse in her womb, a still-life
with sliced fowl—silvery stripes on the walls
marked a distinguished yet obvious absence—
and there were a few pieces of furniture, plus the
                                        nuptial bed
with its immense cover the color of water.
They were together—could touch each other, mix
hair in the same glass, skin in the same scent.
They could chase flames on the curve of their hips,

thrusting kisses where bones met.
But first they should have got rid of the bundles of
death we all carry
placing them carefully on the green tiles of the hearth.

3

Deeply moved he lay at her feet—
in silence. She was watching his hair where
strange pale herbs dried beneath her hands.
She also touched his heart, and was startled
by the urgent rhythms—as if syllables
ran outside the words, and the touch
of his coat still felt strange to her
and beneath it, the shape of his shoulders and chest.
This time no-one had followed them—
except themselves—abandoned and annexed to themselves—
and so, numerous in body and soul, they rested
in a motionless dance.

4

Time and time again she emerged from herself,
until perhaps nakedness,
helped him find his way to her
through the crowd.
He came slowly, undulating, unknown, always nearer,
always meeting, and it seemed that he always
made this journey toward her, through her, to her—
so climbing toward him, she passed on through to find
                                        herself
somewhere beyond them both, yet still meeting him

coming toward her, approaching her, always coming,
                                    always meeting,
—and a great continuity kept them together
till the cry.

5

Late, after midnight, she fell asleep—he didn't.
In her sleep, she heard him breathing a long way off,
like a river at the end of an immense and indifferent
plain. So as not to disturb her, he didn't move, but she,
in moving, touched
his shoulder, familiar now, but cold with night
and from time to time, as he looked at her, she foresaw
the cold night of his gaze.
Bodies returning to bodies, much too young
to become memories, much too old
to misunderstand such beauty.
It was a strong night, a symbol
inhaled very slowly.
The dead held their breath.

6

Then they'd packed everything and fled,
deserting night, and the set in which
the paintings had slowly reappeared; first
the phosphorescent contour of the cat,
then the contour of the mouse within her, then blood,
the screaming blood of birds, the knives glistened.
They ran, ran, but this time
followers could not be stopped. The dead,

once awake, surrounded them
at first invisible but then she was suddenly aware
of a black thread wound
like a thin scar round her left hand, and he
felt his lips mysteriously covered in blood.
They spoke words of love, out loud—but neither heard.
They could no longer hear their own voices, but saw
word shapes freezing in the air.
Then they shouted with eyes—brows—
but neither heard. Their bodies
began to circle slowly, moving away.
The dead became visible, they stumbled into them,
and when lost among them, lost themselves—
never to find each other ever again.

7

And the wolves died,
and the snows melted.
Everything had happened so fast
you'd never have guessed
what had gone on there—with heads and limbs. Even
if you'd asked, they couldn't have told you
where or how those strange nocturnal face stains had
                                        appeared.
In fact how could they know, since by day their faces
were clean and pale, they'd wonder, they'd glance
                                        fleetingly
in the mirror, but too fast to notice
night's greedy eye in the far upper corner, they'd wonder—
then refuse to be questioned any more.

(*BRENDA WALKER AND ANDREA DELETANT*)

III

TABLES WIPED CLEAN

FACE TO FACE

I waited for this moment when, face to face
we are traveling toward a destination which separates us,
face to face, with our features violently reciprocated,
with our hands exhausted by blood,
not daring to kiss, with our clothes not daring to turn red,
with our mouths deserted by that word
that brings day and night into the world.
So, here we are, face to face, becoming more and more
                                        estranged,
alienating ourselves with our whole capacity of
                                misunderstanding,
in a true species' adversity—so that,
when the train jerks us into each other's arms
we have the revelation of death
as, probably the mammoths had
when they leapt into the next era.

(*Brenda Walker and Andrea Deletant*)

OF NO USE

No. You've never needed my gestures
tied up like ribbons round some handle,
or my eyes embroidered on the fixtures,
or my whole playful universe.

You never needed that heavenly bliss
of words—or the absolute yearning
whose pale chisel carved
the stone of moments into the shape of a kiss.

I was no use to you—it was like seasons that pass
in reverse, twos, threes or fours,
like rain trying to fill a glass,
or ruining books when it pours.

(*BRENDA WALKER AND ANDREA DELETANT*)

ESCAPE

He locked me in: his love—a prison.
His words and looks—padlocks.
I became blind and mute,
could no longer tell
a curtain from a river;
ashen grass, dead hair invaded me,
dead nails grew on my fingers,
a bluish skin covered my eyes.
I could no longer tell
a bracelet from a muzzle,
a wagon from a cello,
I was speechless—couldn't even answer
the call of the pomegranate seed,
or that kind invitation of frogs in the sunset,
I wasn't even able to say "hello,"
—I lost a lot of friends.

Then suddenly, I noticed
my cheeks had become hollow to the touch,
my hands uneven,
the body was entering its sheath
—and, realizing all this, with the speed of disgust
I cut off the dead nails,
excoriated my artificial eyes,
broke the lock
and ran out.
There was no guard.
No one to raise the alarm.
No one called out after me.
No one begged me to return.
Not a soul greeted me.
No one.

(*BRENDA WALKER AND ANDREA DELETANT*)

COLD

Cold. Necessary cold
raising the first protuberances: the mountains,
sons and daughters of cold,
tamed then to the first vegetal feeling,
to the first call of an eye,
to the first unbalanced ape
—to humanity.

When the snake's tongue parts
—it's getting cold.
Cold is the result of divergence.
I stretch my hand—and something withdraws
or, if I still touch it,
contracts itself abruptly
becoming dark and crouched.
Something moves away leaving a trace of cold,
something always abandons its place
leaving behind a cold space,
something separates from something
in the great analytical moment.

Cold has no shadow.
His contour doesn't allow him this evasion.
Shadow is form's feeling.
Cold has no feeling.
He's immutable, self-centered, he doesn't communicate.

On the table—two glasses
and two parallel spoons.
At the table, two parallel people
watching the street.
A man and a woman
or a woman and a man
—you can't tell

because they don't attract one another.
I dilate myself—to fill up the conventional space
                              between people.
To take revenge, they try to crush me, anyway
they have to touch me and, if I step away,
they collide with each other, touch each other,
having no choice, they yell at each other,
and so end up addressing each other,
willy-nilly they notice themselves and their similarities,
and that happens at the surface of the massacre, in the open,
or higher still at the level of conscience
—who could name the place where something begins to
                              change?

Cold's lifestyle produces a strange impression of order.
In fact, under conventional lines,
I suspect a wild movement,
everyone his teeth clenched into another's carotid,
nails thrust into another's flesh;
under the plate of cold
a daily massacre takes place,
a hunger which has lost its meaning,
a competition which has lost its sense,
and the more the turmoil turns vicious,
the more distinguished conventional lines appear,
like a draft traced with chalk on a blackboard
which looks so much like a ghost.

Cold between stars, people,
cold bisecting couples with lines
—and in between, an infinite net of conventions
(reminders of ideas and sentiments
or projections of ideas and sentiments
—things are mixed up), as for the laws,

the laws flow in an invisible, implacable way, beyond
                                    cold and warmth,
so that this small, circumstantial law—the convention—
seems suddenly friendly and sailing—after all
she is the one who asks for our handshake,
for uttering "good day" and "good night,"
she, the convention, the pale, sweet sister of the law,
making it easier for us, if not to live,
at least, to survive.

(*Brenda Walker and Andrea Deletant*)

A HAPPENING

Yesterday I watched an amazing fight
between a woman in love and a man
who wasn't, her hair agitated,
and her mouth interrupted by white teeth.
She talked and talked—he didn't. She talked furiously,
striking expired time with words.
There was no sound of shields.
Time totally disarmed!
She had her arguments, he did not.
He was leaving her for another woman;
he was guilty—so was the other woman,
but the woman who loved was the innocent party.
Her words had a natural nobleness,
the mud of passion left only cast gold.
To avoid her eyes, he looked at his hands—
noticing a certain contrast between them.

It was a ridiculously unfair battle,
the air whistled as if clutching a line
of a thousand arrows never reaching their target.

Everything about them seemed to sink—to decline.

(BRENDA WALKER AND ANDREA DELETANT)

THE YOUNG BAT

To begin, he circled my neck shyly
and laced it with his singing;
I almost fell in love with his ugly
triangular head, his squinting eyes,
and the sound of his frail bones.

At his first bite
I felt a great relief.
My pulse throbbed eagerly
knowing my blood would flow, diluted,
into another goitre, absolved of sin.

Then I grew weaker.
Clamped to my neck, the vampire
was drinking me, drinking me constantly.
His wings flared wide and free,
his eyes burned like two hieroglyphs—
but I couldn't decipher the message.

(CHRISTOPHER HEWITT)

THE BLOOD

Ah, how well I remember that pain!
My soul taken by surprise
jumped about like a chicken with its head cut off.
Everything was splashed with blood, the street, the café table,
especially your thoughtless hands.
Strewn about, my hair wandered
like a monster among the glasses,
coiled around them as if around suspended breaths
then danced, vertical, whistling,
and fell, executed, at your feet.
Ah, how well I remember that I smiled savagely,
disfiguring myself so as to look more like myself,
and that I cried only once,
long after everyone had left
and the lights were out and the tables
had been wiped clean of the blood.

(MARGUERITE DORIAN AND ELLIOTT URDANG)

SHE WAS BEAUTIFUL AND WICKED

She was beautiful and wicked.
He was wicked and beautiful.
From head to toe
they were smeared with viper honey.

She was afraid of goodness.
Of goodness he was afraid.
Shields of sin
guarded him, guarded her.

They lived in ignorance.
They died in ignorance.
The saints still sorrow
in the silver icon.

(LAURA SCHIFF)

ROMANCE

Forgive me for making you weep,
I should have murdered you,
I should have dragged out your soul
and battered you with it.

I should have watched your blood
flow, surge after surge,
and left your puny, pockmarked self alone,
not caressed your eyes, nostrils and mouth.

Forgive me for making you suffer,
I should have terrified you,
But I'm not God—the avenger
—only his creation of dust.

(BRENDA WALKER AND ANDREA DELETANT)

LIKE GULLIVER

Like Gulliver who towed a hundred ships,
I drag you to the shore, my motley lovers,
so artful, all with rapiers at your hips,
and bent on war, so many silly rovers.

Like Gulliver I spare you all, although
you hit my forehead, hoping it will crack;
I laugh at you through streaks of blood,—oh, you,
my savage lovers, avid to attack.

(PETRE SOLOMON)

THANKS

I can't take it—you're so handsome!
And when night falls your hair shimmers
grand and tragic like the echo
of blood on a shield.
Your eyes make the air pulse,
they electrify the house,
the drawers open, rugs flood
down the stairs like a river.
Your star-like teeth
rip open my heart like lightning.
I can't stand it—you're too much!

But look, thanks for your low forehead.
It gives me more leisure to spend
on those beautiful lips, those treacherous teeth.

(LAURA SCHIFF)

THE GOOD OLD HABITS

The family life that you've enjoyed,
My pretty pithecanthropoid,
On the whole, is rather fine:
So weep no more, sweet baby mine.

With conjugal pleasure never wanting,
Your home is such a happy nest:
Your caveman husband's mad for hunting,
His bloody weapons never rest.

Every third day without fail,
He drags you in some sweet wagtail,
Which, going wild at the sight of you,
Leaves your bare breasts black and blue.

With blissful hours thus employed,
My good wife pithecanthropoid,
Your life is daily on the line:
So weep no more, sweet baby mine.

(WILLIAM JAY SMITH)

ORCHESTRA

Climbing the scales three octaves at a time,
I search for you among the high notes where
the tender flute resides. But where are your
sweet eyelashes? Not there.

Then I descend among the sunlit brasses—
their funnels glistening like fountain tips.
I let them splash me with their streaming gold,
but I can't find your lips.

Then daring ever deeper I explore
the depths the elemental strings command.
Their bows will not create a miracle
without your stroking hand.

The orchestra is still. The score is blank.
Cold as a slide rule the brasses, strings, and flute.
Sonorous lover, when will you return?
The orchestra is mute.

(DANA GIOIA)

PRIDE

I have no time to offer proof to you
of the great, astonishing virtues I possess; therefore,
those who have eyes will see; to those who do not see,
my eyes will remain undiscovered as before.

Some there are who, meeting me, have said:
"Welcome to my life, you living wonder!"
Other had nothing whatever to say to me,
and I left them far behind, wanting upward to wander.

Time sweeps on, and I have precious gifts,
and I constantly seek out those who merit them.
If I do not find them, then let me be buried
like a paraoh, with my riches, so the Earth may inherit them.

(PETRE SOLOMON)

PROJECT OF WISDOM

Even now I know the hour when
I'll rummage through dozens of drawers for you,
so I can tell someone how much I loved
when young.
I'll have letters and photos
stacks of looks, gestures crushed alive,
and my hands will flutter among them
like dried leaves.

But I'll tell, I'll tell how you smiled beside me
by my soft, sweet lips,
how you knew we'd be one, always,
forever, or till death.

And I'll tell of your profile
melting its thin frame in the light,
the eyes mottled like two huge insects
caught in the April rain.

O someone will surely praise.
"Yes, you had an extraordinary feast of love . . ."
I'll close the drawers.
Even now I know the hour when . . .

(LAURA SCHIFF)

SAND

My hands creep forward on the hot sand
to unknown destinations;
perhaps to the shoreline,
perhaps to the arms from which they were severed
and which lie on the beach
like two decapitated eels.

(NAOMI LAZARD)

MORNING EXERCISES

I wake up and say: I'm through.
It's my first thought at dawn.
What a nice way to start the day
with such a murderous thought.

God, take pity on me
—is the second thought, and then
I get out of bed
and live as if
nothing had been said.

(BRENDA WALKER AND ANDREA DELETANT)

LADY OF MIRACLES

Since you walked out on me
I'm getting lovelier by the hour.
I glow like a corpse in the dark.
No one sees how round and sharp
my eyes have grown
how my carcass looks like a glass urn,
how I hold up things in the rags of my hands,
the way I can stand though crippled by lust.
No, there's just your cruelty circling
my head like a bright rotting halo.

(*LAURA SCHIFF*)

WITH A THIN PENCIL OF PLATINUM

With a thin pencil of platinum
the moon underlines the horizon.
But I have lied.
The daughter of the moon is a liar.
When it is cold on earth,
a stripe of light is not enough
to underline our existence.

(LAURA SCHIFF)

GHOST

A rug of dead butterflies at my feet,
dead and limp
(they don't experience rigor mortis).
I, on the other hand, am quite healthy:
I've extracted my liver,
plucked out my lungs,
wrenched out my heart,
and nothing hurts anymore.

To become a ghost
is a solution
I weakly recommend.

(*CHRISTOPHER HEWITT*)

MUD

The scales which cover me
are the color of earth
like a crocodile
adapted to the surrounding mud,
motionless—eyes appearing asleep,
inside—ferocious.

The insignificant animal ought to beware of me.
Look at it hopping around,
its hairy muzzle touching my back.
I feel my jaws clenching
ready to open
into that great murderous yawn.

Nothing happens.
I'm just an old woman.

(BRENDA WALKER AND ANDREA DELETANT)

THE WIDOW

The cold has gnarled her fingers,
the heat has blistered her arms.
The weather has reached her brain
and turned it into a storm cloud.
She wears no black veils,
no fur or feathers, but creeps
naked like a lizard.
She is ugly.
A dog sniffs at her solitude
and takes off yelping.
She smells
incitingly
of absence.

(CHRISTOPHER HEWITT)

IV

THE WHEEL
NOT IN MY
HANDS

THE CRIPPLES

When the cripples hurl their crutches in the air
the sticks beat our heads, our sound heads.
Yet only we rush to grab them
a second before they topple,
we who stand bruised
till they stop whimpering,
these cripples draped in our arms.
They stain us with urine,
they gouge us, they sigh
in our ear something obscene.
and we keep propping them up.
But if we had never meddled
we'd see them running, flying,
jeering, hopping agilely on one leg,
snatching their tumbling crutches—
the crutches they'd die without—
for what else can they hit with?

(*LAURA SCHIFF*)

THE GREEN ELEPHANT

Come, come close to the window.
I present you with a model
of the universe.

Let's inspect these trophies
and this fine collection of guillotines
with the blood wiped off

and the proud tusk of the Green Elephant
which I shot once from a low angle
in a moment of cowardice and screaming.
Despite the confusion, I still recall
the bow of his colossal knee.

Examine carefully these coins and
handkerchiefs of dead queens
from rainy towns
and this skull with its enormous
sad eye sockets resting uncomfortably
on its crossbones.

It shouldn't come as a surprise to you
that after such a great feat
there was no proper reward.
These injustices are quite common.
But come.
Come close to the window.

(CHRISTOPHER HEWITT)

DEAD STILL

The wheel is not in my hands.
The wheel is over my head;
no one turns it left
or right: the vessel is dead still.
The wheel rests like a spider
fixed on my wooden sky.
What is it doing up there?
It's a helm gone mad.
What could it possibly steer
on the vertical road of the Nowhere Sea?
And why does the helm not move
in this world so rich in helmsmen?
The wind at least could have set it in motion.
Where is the somnambulant bat to give it a turn?
Where is the moon to alter its shape,
lengthen the spokes and flatten the contour
so that it is more of a fish?
The vessel's voyage must end here:
the helm is insane, it cannot steer.

(WILLIAM JAY SMITH)

THE BEAR

The bear paces the cage for hours
the four bars in the four corners
drip with his saliva and sniffs
the bear's snout up and down on
the four bars, only the four bars
a frenzy for four sides.
If the cage were completely round
he'd stand in the center for hours
feeling all points narrowing tight
to a prison and at last he'd lose
the tragic illusion of a road along
one side and from there again along
another side and from there again along
another side and from there, again . . .

(LAURA SCHIFF)

AGORAPHOBIA

I find I'm in Daedalus' labyrinth.
I know a thousand exits.
I know the hideous secret.
I don't want to leave! My limbs are thin
like those of a young goat
I secreted out of myself.

There are unhinging winding worlds
and the corner of the evening panic.
Perhaps I'm meant to die a too intimate death.
Only not outside!
not outside!

(LAURA SCHIFF)

A DREAM OF DROUGHT

Water's getting dearer.
I'd better learn
To swim in dust
And drink mud.

Birds leave in the autumn
And don't return in the spring.

Blue cloth's getting dearer.
I'd better get used
To wearing black.

Even fish scales of any size
Have registered a rise!

(BRENDA WALKER AND ANDREA DELETANT)

THE RABBIT

The rabbit
    who invented that shriek
    to elicit the hunter's compassion
    though neither hunter nor dog
    was ever deterred from
    snatching up his body
    like a fur glove
    warm from recent wearing
The rabbit
    who could only invent that shriek
    (far bolder than his own anatomy)
    to confront Death
The rabbit
    whose excruciating ludicrous shriek
    is his only notion of solemnity

(CHRISTOPHER HEWITT)

THE DOORS

The open doors and beyond are seen
fruit and leaves and puddles and cats.
The door ajar and one sees
other doors, rain, stones and a pair
of greenish slippers like two long ears;
open doors facing other open doors
between them a dangerous intimate zone
and he who tried to cross
never made it—
and again fruit and puddles of water,
and the snail sun drags its light
over all the lives swallowed in the void
between two open doors,
and we, endlessly, stubbornly see
only stones, leaves, slippers, cats . . .

(LAURA SCHIFF)

EXORCISM

I'm not afraid of the angel-fowl
preening their innocent wings
in the windy light. I'm not disturbed
by the female Alcyone. I don't shudder
at the avalanche of bodies cast on the
Tarpeian Rock and all that raked flesh.
Alphabets don't scare me—
even the A raised on its crutches
doesn't bother me, nor do the ropes
of rain which throttle the souls
of young girls. I'm not afraid
of the roads where rabbits make
sudden appearances smiling like
fur-clad buddhas, or of the chanting
that breeds assassins, or of the
torture of the imaginary numbers.
Monday (Sunday's conscience) holds
no fear for me, neither does the
long visit of the Man who was Thursday.
I don't dread the sinister key to
the Door to Beyond worn transparent
by endless knocking like the
skin of a drum to the thinness of air.
The nacelle doesn't alarm me (it sounds
like the name of a flower), nor would I
be afraid if the Solar System twisted
off its axis. I don't fear the whiff
of glaciers or the anemic skin of the
Valley of Reflection slit dagger-like
by the River of Life, or the microbes
of sugar, or the joints on the eighty fingers
of a water sprite, or the donkeys which
St. Mary sent forth into the world,
or that venemous old woman Cunegonda.

No, no, I'm not afraid, not afraid
of Gomorrah or the Island of Ré:
Felix qui potuit rerum cognoscere causas.

(CHRISTOPHER HEWITT)

SACRILEGE

I ate the tongue of the stag,
the thick stag-tongue that used
to lick the foliage, the brook;
on it I munched, amused.

I ate the flesh of the stag,
the virile flesh at his throat.
I consumed his heart, and then
on his antlers hung my raincoat.

While the hooves, the nostrils, and the skin—
all unpalatable—
lay scattered all around,

still bleeding on the ground.

(PETRE SOLOMON AND WILLIAM JAY SMITH)

FABLE

An angel had its wing cut off.
Try to fly anyhow, said God,
try to fly anyhow,
even if you can't be graceful—
aesthetics doesn't matter here,
only your ability to master imbalance.
It's one of my experiments on angels.

Said and done.
The angel plummeted
through frost and light,
his feathers carbonized,
his sole wing
impotent,
dangling.
Eventually, burning with speed,
he landed on a roof.

Feet, hands, face
flushed with blood.

Looking up, the people
said: "Oh, there's a stork!"

(CHRISTOPHER HEWITT)

POSTMERIDIAN

1

After the morning has cut the sediment of night
with luminous acids, here is the afternoon
slowly recovering, getting heavier,
feeding on the general tiredness.
Here is the afternoon with its look
of a middle-aged woman who once
committed a crime, long ago,
never discovered, forgotten, of no consequence;
she now passes, always unnoticed.
Most people sleep, or feel, even
while still at work, their gestures slow motion.
The afternoon passes among them, through them,
moving its heavy haunches.

2

The great rest, the great parties, the great solitudes
take place at night, when one possesses time,
when, after work, time finds itself
in the man in the North Railway Station,
in the woman in the South Railway Station,
in the deaf-mutes in the restaurant,
whose quiet liveliness does not contaminate anyone,
in a certain nuptial room,
in a certain attitude of sleep,
in a particular dream in the shape of a rhombus.

3

The afternoon is intermediary time.
Those who love lack the courage to show themselves.

Those who are loved let themselves be waited for.
Waiting expands chairs,
flattens the telephone,
the walls become pneumatic;
you hit your head against them in vain; it doesn't hurt—
the entire universe is anesthetized.

Those who love ring the doorbell, and when you open
there is nobody there; somebody ran away leaving behind
a delicate ectoplasm which disappears
if you breathe too heavily.
And so, between those who left and those who did not come,
you stand frozen, disfigured,
tattooed on the air.

4

In the afternoon, the cobras sleep.
In their long slumber only the venom stays awake,
like a violet light bulb.
The lions with their wise jaws sleep.
In the sky, the pale soul of the stars.
In the alphabet, the letter "M," the letter "N,"
closely embraced, sleep.

5

Postmeridian—take care:
day is half gone; you've already forgotten
the sparkling thorns of sunrise;
the speed of light in the tree's spine
now has passed its peak.

After the cold waters of dawn sculpted you,
experience was deposited on your body
in thin layers, invisible.

6

If you could live
the tea hours, the coffee hours,
the tranquil sound of cups,
if you could conceive of the fragile amber hours,
the afternoon of an old family in an old century
altered by a romantic memory,
if only you would resist the horror
of seeing your face in the cupful
of tea, burning in the flames of Hell.

Or, in the later afternoon hours,
have you ever seen the sudden rain of wrinkles
falling on your visitor's cheek?
It is as if the light's decline
would first test its victim,
then abandon it without going for the kill,
leaving it terrorized for the rest of its life.
And you who watch say nothing,
only ask yourself if the same mass of wrinkles,
like a living creature, didn't throb for an instant
on your own face. You do something, anything—
for example, light a cigarette—
and, finally, twilight saves you.

Finally, the air is cool, like the body after love.
The vapors of premonition are lost.
The afternoon moves to the other side of the globe,

with its aspect of a middle-aged woman,
each hand carrying a loaded shopping bag.
Who knows what they contain? Maybe flour,
    maybe raw meat.
In any case, some bloody streaks were observed
    in her wake,
in the railway station, in the lion's eye,
in the cup of tea. Don't worry about it now.
From the newspapers, tomorrow,
we'll find out what really happened.

(CRISTIAN ANDREI, NAOMI LAZARD, AND NINA CASSIAN)

FAIRYTALE

—Why is it that the ugliest of the ugly,
the most hideous of the hideous—wants to be called
                              Prince Charming?
—But, answered the Princess, what befits a disguise?
What if inside that scabby toad there lies bewitched
the wonderful Prince himself?
That's a risk I dare not take.

And the Princess kissed his warts
and took him to bed.
And the scabby toad croaked—
satisfied.

(BRENDA WALKER AND ANDREA DELETANT)

THAT ANIMAL

That animal was tamed by me.
I extracted it from chaos;
I smeared it
with the pale unction of my kindness.

And then it swallowed me!
What a foul muzzle!
How unworthy its bowels!

You hear me, Jonah?

(CHRISTOPHER HEWITT)

THE CATERPILLAR

The enormous green caterpillar,
nourished on rain
and on leaf-blood,
the giant caterpillar with its bristling hairs,
whose head is one great snout,
whose violet antennae
troubled the air—
the storm hurled it on my table
one early evening
when the cold came down,
obliging me to watch it
drag itself along, unconscious
of the threat it held for me,
but tenacious in its movement
toward me, the caterpillar
with its electric flesh,
that approached me with determined slowness,
entering forever
into my orbit,
fat, green, wet, and blind.

(WILLIAM JAY SMITH)

ARGUING WITH CHAOS

My visitors are:
a gentleman interrupted at the waist,
a continuous lady
and their tin daughter,
a teacher who professes cheese,
an assassin with the flu, a lot of
unmarried termites,
a tree with a mustache,
a young stork,
a child with a cardboard leg,
and three people ignorant of the laws of kinetics.

At last appears
the evening hound
that barks very loud
and drives them out.

(WILLIAM JAY SMITH AND CRISTIAN ANDREI)

THE BIG-BILLED SWAN

If on a clear night
you linger here,
the big-billed swan
will surely appear.

Wait for a second;
then no doubt
from one of her wings
an arm will sprout.

Don't fall asleep;
just leave her alone:
she'll soon be half-woman
and only half-swan.

While under starlight
her white feathers glide,
moonlight will mold
her white skinside.

Do not panic,
but patiently stay
till into the dark
she drifts away.

(WILLIAM JAY SMITH)

IT FRIGHTENS ME

My aunt's needle, through whose eye
a long, rough, white thread penetrates,
frightens me.
Any eye pierced by a thread frightens me,
also the clacking of the flat bills of those
who come to warn us about something terrible,
and the fly's body, its flickering legs,
the black segments that rub against each other.

The dark event will occur in any case
but for now, through fear alone,
I postpone my destiny.

(NAOMI LAZARD)

THE SYLLABLES OF THE LIE

I am reading your lips
as they form the syllables of a lie.
A glass-blower,
you breathe into the vitreous magma—
and there they are: fruit, vegetables,
threatening animals.
Your lips at times rolled back to show your teeth,
in ever-increasing arrogance,
teeming with a myriad organisms,
some on cilia, some on stilts.

(WILLIAM JAY SMITH)

AND WHEN SUMMER COMES TO AN END

And when summer comes to an end
it's like the world coming to an end.
Wilderness and terror—everywhere!

Days shrink
till all dignity's gone.
Wet slabs of cloth
drape our bodies:
dejected coats.
And then we shiver, stumbling
into the holes of Winter Street
on the corner of Decline . . .

What's the good of living
with the idea of Spring
—dangerous as any Utopia?

(BRENDA WALKER AND ANDREA DELETANT)

HUMAN

Sometimes I see very clearly the snout of the beast
opening below me. I can count the fangs,
see the blood-red glottis shivering with greed,
see its fixed eyes full of an unquelled instinct.

I sit perched in the tree, hesitating,
rocked this way and that
by my feelings,
weakened by ideas,
and I know I won't be able to hold out
unless, breaking loose from myself,
I recover my flawless instinct,
the one that makes of me a single claw
clutching the tree; and I cannot do it
and I fall, full of memories and images,
savoring my life and my death
up to the instant when my forehead shatters.

(MARGUERITE DORIAN AND ELLIOTT URDANG)

V

LIFE
SENTENCE

WHAT I TOLD THE SQUIRREL

I saved you from the anonymity of the leaves,
from the hazel's mediocre refuge.
I hurled you into the light,
naming you bushy red,
deciding on your leap and on your goal.
Everything you do belongs to me
even if you suddenly try
to swim through the gravel
or to nibble huge chunks of cardboard
or suddenly to open and close
those mechanical eyes of yours:
you cannot confuse me,
you cannot escape from my poem's prison.

(WILLIAM JAY SMITH)

A FAMOUS WOMAN

Lady Macbeth had a goal,
Lady Macbeth had a vision.
Preparing for an essential birth,
totally barren she remained.

If instead of her clear vision
she had merely had offspring,
who would ever have heard of her?

(WILLIAM JAY SMITH)

EXTRAORDINARY PERFORMANCE

He held up both his arms,
a rose in one, in the other,
a flute pierced
by a sweet marrow of sound,
and he danced.
Then barely moving his hands,
he sketched cities
and ground out slender shrieks of water.
(Backstage
all the switches on the control board were being operated.)
So he invented the steam engine and draped
himself in an invisible cloak
on which algae were painted, green on green.
Then he ate, drank, and suddenly
became a fairy maiden
and swore love to everyone present.

In the end the applause was weak.

The monkey fell back on all fours.

(WILLIAM JAY SMITH)

SELF-PORTRAIT

I was given at birth this odd triangular
face, the sugared cone that you see now,
the figurehead jutting from some pirate prow,
framed by trailing strands of moonlike hair.

Disjointed shape I'm destined to carry around
and thrust out steadily through endless days,
wounding the retinas of those who gaze
on the twisted shadow I cast upon the ground.

Disowned by the family from which I came,
who am I? Earth conspires to turn me back,
the white race and the yellow, the redskin and the black,
till even to the species I lay little claim.

And only when—a self-inflicted woman—
I cry out; only when I face the cold;
and only when by time I'm stained and soiled
do they find me beautiful: and call me human.

(WILLIAM JAY SMITH)

FARCE

Allow me to rearrange my bones—
those awkward obstacles
blocking my flesh,

leading it, forcing it into
a pear (my woman's shape)
or starfish (my hands).

Allow my bones to
try out new geometries—
the outline of the world's first
schooner, or the transparent
skeleton of a lily,
or the genealogical tree
with its posthumous fruit,
its final offspring barren.

Allow my bones to kneel down
when I pretend to pray,
so that the Kind Paleontologist
will be fooled at least once!

(CHRISTOPHER HEWITT)

SOFTENING, SOFTENING

And softening, softening
nature's angles,
I've gained a lovely, earthly globe
but lost the mountains, forests
and other reliefs.
What can I do with this perfection
that's plugged the ravine
and erased all differences of color?
I shut my eyes, my finger taps the globe
randomly.
Maybe I touched a man.
Maybe touched him exactly on the forehead.
I test the sea with my finger.
I feel neither coolness
nor the bite of the shark.
What can I do with this perfection,
silent, boxed between the two antipodes
of self-love?

(*LAURA SCHIFF*)

JOYFUL SACRIFICE

Devour the earth and its waters
and such flesh as
remains on our bones
after calamity!

Eat up the elements of the world,
rinse out your mouth with the sky,
and like a pippin spit out the moon,
any moon,
no moon.

Ghostly devourers, consume
the constellation "Brothers and Sisters,"
devour it down to the bone.
Do you not love our nervous system?

We do love it, have loved it,
from generations of rutting plants,
stumbling against the final obstacle, the absolute.

(BARBARA HOWES AND KIM CUSHMAN)

TO MY CRITICS

Tin-ear will shout:
Don't mumble! Speak out!

Lame-leg will bray:
Cart that poet away!

Dumb Dodo drums along,
demanding a song.

Pure Fool then will bellow
for something to follow.

To Lazy Son-of-a-bitch
I'm asleep at the switch.

They all bicker madly
to be served so badly
with all my life,
with all my life.

(WILLIAM JAY SMITH)

TIRADE FOR THE NEXT-TO-LAST ACT

I'm leaving you, I won't touch you anymore.
I've run out of things I have to prove to you,
so there's no reason to postpone the drowning
of molecules called hands or eyes or mouth
in the patient earth which waits—but not for me.
Earth knows it owns me, right to horizon-zero.
I've told you almost everything I know;
even the lie I told was a pious lie
because it leapt to life, came into being
embodied as a leaf, or as a rabbit,
and I cannot reject a living creature.
Also, I leave you because I am so weary
of the way the century melts in the one before
as if the milk the child sucks from its mother
went back into her breast—or worse than that,
as if the brow of a philosopher
kept sloping back till it rejoined a species
long extinct, and hirsute, and prehensile.

I've picked up information on my way
but none of it from scholarly pursuits
or from the established canon of great books;
mostly from heat and cold, from birth and death,
all that comes past us only once, alas,
so it's no guide for what will happen next.
I remain as vulnerable as ever,
knowing a thousand objects by their names,
a thousand states of mind I cannot name.
I don't see their utter metamorphoses,
I didn't notice when they took their leave,
abandoning me to confusion,
as if dropped into a pool of blood.
So I'm leaving; I won't touch you anymore.
You've said so many times you can't abide me

though I drew my portrait for you with such care,
relying on the way you had sketched it out.
But I'm incapable of imitation,
or so it seems. I lack the talent
to resemble you—much less, myself.

My smiles are always misconstrued as grins,
And when I laugh, all heads are turned away
as if I had committed some indecency.
I pick the wrong occasions for my tears:
when the crowd cheers a city holiday.
When I sculpt a statue, everyone screams,
"He has made himself into a graven image!"
When I shrivel with a serious illness,
I'm not believed: it's the devious way
my sad body causes an obscure epidemic . . .
So I'm leaving you, goodbye. Goodbye, I leave.

(CAROLYN KIZER)

THE KIWI BIRD

I am the Kiwi bird
the one without wings . . .
Don't speak to me,
Don't call me.
I don't understand you . . .
Because I can't fly
and because some children
throw stones at me
I've become dumb.
My beak opens sometimes by itself,
as if I were thirsty
as if I were sick,
but I'm neither sick nor thirsty.
I am only dumb,
very very dumb.
Other times, however,
I think I hear something,
something like the flapping of a sheet in the wind,
or a wing in flight,
and then I walk a little
I raise my stiff leg
and my step seems suddenly alert
but I immediately sit down on the ground
and with my long beak,
I begin to scratch my wingless back
scratch, scratching as if
there were nothing left in the world
but me and my beak that pokes.
I'm the Kiwi bird that can't understand.
Don't speak to me,
Don't call me.
Once every few years, it happens
when the moon seems to hum, and ring in a certain way
that shame and sorrow, my only emotions

start glimmering in my flesh,
and then I want to hide
and I have nowhere,
and I twist and bend
and I have nothing with which to cover myself.

I am the Kiwi bird
the one without wings.

I am the Kiwi bird.

(LAURA SCHIFF)

NIGHT MUST FALL

I was walking one evening on a country road.
It was a dry spring without fragrance,
and my footsteps were muffled by the dust.
Such strange scenery! I said to myself, watching
the motionless branches, the earth
still unruffled by even the premonition of grass.
The light was calm.

Suddenly on the horizon there appeared
a form: gross, heavy, tenacious.
Was it a cloud shaped like a camel?
I asked an invisible Polonius.
When the form grew nearer—
it was an ox.
It was a quiet ox
sinking its silent hooves in the dust,
with its skin the color of stone,
with its bleached symmetrical horns,
with its square forehead.

I hoped for an instant—only for an instant—
that I was wrong, that I would make out
the reassuringly full maternal udders
or else recognize the virile muscular neck
of a bull. But it was useless.
It was only a neutered, passionless ox.

He stopped in front of me. He looked at me—
the wise white ox.
The falling evening framed the countryside.
I tried to avoid that messenger of solitude
by walking on through the dust.
But turning after me, with its indifferent stare,
serene death followed.

(DANA GIOIA)

POINT OF VIEW

The Courtyard is filled with allegories,
the wood with fables.
The animals have vanished,
the world has vanished.
What's left?
The arrogant Weltanschauung.

(CHRISTOPHER HEWITT)

REPETITIO

A blade of grass
a curved blade of grass,
curved like an eyelash, a blade of grass,
a blade of grass piercing the earth,
sweetening its desert,
a blade of grass counting out my seasons,
one by one,
four by four,
waiting calmly for me to become
a blade of grass,
a blade of grass.

(NINA CASSIAN)

THE AFTER LIFE

About all these I write freely
but all these terrorize me.
I name a seagull
and its shadow covers me
and the shadow of its beak drills at my skull
and a shadow of blood runs down my cheek.
I say "hunger" or "goodbye"
and "hunger" makes my eyes drown in their sockets,
"hunger" melts my chest and womb,
comes "goodbye" and tears my love,
"goodbye" pries open my arms
and makes everything fall to the ground.

In writing them down, I wanted to free them
but all they can do is grab and devour;
all these feel free only by killing.
They do not believe in the Poem's after life.

(CRISTIAN ANDREI)

PLEASE GIVE THIS SEAT TO AN ELDERLY OR DISABLED PERSON

I stood during the entire journey:
nobody offered me a seat
although I was at least a hundred years older than anyone else on
    board,
although the signs of at least three major afflictions
were visible on me:
Pride, Loneliness, and Art.

(NAOMI LAZARD)

ORBITS

The orbit I describe in my environment,
cautiously, so as not to strike birds with my forehead,
tables, or the elegant plants, merciless
on their steel armatures;
                    the way I pass, hissing
over the compact waters whose interior maw
is ready to suck me in, near dangerous statues
whose kaleidoscopic eyes are moving
in their empty sockets at certain hours;
the orbit my body follows
through deformed objects which I manage to avoid
despite their unpredictable contours,
my arm in danger every moment
of being ripped from shoulder to the tip of forefinger,
            the extremity that precedes me,
            the part that indicates distances;
any moment my hip can be severed;
my orbit continues, that whirligig
whose meaning I used to know, forgot
            and from time to time remember
when I pass very close to a primordial event—
then I thrill like a carniverous flower
            shaken out of indifference
            when an object touches its petals;
at which time the notions of *beginning, end, right, left,*
forward, backward become perfectly clear to me
            for that moment alone;
then my orbit possesses me once more:
my only care is to avoid striking the vertebrae
of the giant saurians who are constantly being exhumed
in vaster and vaster numbers, not to be impaled
on the blue spire of a skyscraper, not to be swallowed
by the wave-functions that crisscross
            the matrix of the universe:

however, who can tell?—it is possible
that I am immobile and surrounded by orbits,
that the wind which ruffles my hair
is caused by the rapid passage of a flying table,
a statue rushing by—or it is possible
that we are all turning in our orbits
trying to avoid a collision course,
the crash occurring just when an object
loses the instinct of its own nature,
the plant that of a plant,
the wave that of a wave,
the bird that of a bird,
and me—of mine.

(NAOMI LAZARD)

THREE PRIESTS

Singing, they walked upon the water,
three priests who prayed improperly,
employing always the wrong words,
but never provoking God's rage or sorrow.
They floated by so beautifully—
the three in ignorance complete—
that Divine Law itself bowed down
and kissed the soles of their wet feet.

(WILLIAM JAY SMITH)

POETRY

From this pencil departs a path of black lead
and along it a letter like a dog makes its way—
and here is a word, an inhabited homestead,
which I may reach tomorrow or the following day.

(WILLIAM JAY SMITH)

MY PARENTS BENT OVER A BOOK

A thunderstorm attacks the city;
hail dances on young trees—it's a merry disaster.
The window's cornea splits
as my parents, bent together over a book,
arrange words in a particular order.
My mother has lost her eyebrows;
my father's hands are small and swollen.
My parents transpose hail into syllables,
tear away the water from the open book
over and over again, more and more tired
they rescue the book from the flood,
the paper, heavy and sodden as a tent,
struggles in the high wind,
sometimes slapping my father's forehead,
in which case, my mother discovers
an unexpected strength to discipline the paper.

(NAOMI LAZARD)

VOWEL

A clean vowel
is my morning,
Latin pronunciation
in the murmur of confused time.
With rational syllables
I'm trying to clear the occult mind
and promiscuous violence.
My linguistic protest
has no power.
The enemy is illiterate.

(BRENDA WALKER AND ANDREA DELETANT)

LICENTIOUSNESS

Letters fall from my words
as teeth might fall from my mouth.
Lisping? Stammering? Mumbling?
Or the last silence?
Please God take pity
on the roof of my mouth,
on my tongue,
on my glottis,
on the clitoris in my throat
vibrating, sensitive, pulsating,
exploding in the orgasm of Romanian.

BRENDA WALKER AND ANDREA DELETANT)

SPELL

Write, write, write
fly, bright kite
sing, sweet string—
tie up everything—
write, write, write.

Stiff in his collar
sits a fine scholar,
cold quill at rest
on his palimpsest—
write, write, write.

As if in a gale
a giant whale
swallows all myth
and leaves us here with
an empty shell—
write, write, write.

Writing's a game
that's never the same:
Alfred writes Alpha
Betty writes Beta
Mama writes Gamma
while I write Pi—
paper-white
tombstone-white—
write, write, write.

(WILLIAM JAY SMITH)

20
28 30 31 33 35
GREED 26
(44)   65

54 Symbolism 57 - 58
   61 Romance
      figurative

87 sacrilej